Landmark
B O O K S

Robert E. Lee

AND THE ROAD OF HONOR

ROBERT E. LEE

AND THE

ROAD OF HONOR

★

by HODDING CARTER

Illustrated by

WILLIAM HUTCHINSON

RANDOM HOUSE · NEW YORK

This book is about a great American who was guided by something he believed to be the most precious quality in life. It is called a sense of honor, a force inside us which not only tells us what is the right thing for us to do but also impels us to do it. Robert Edward Lee of Virginia, who led the armies of the seceding South in the war for Southern independence, walked straight on honor's road all his life.

Contents

1

The Arsenal at Harpers Ferry

If you had been a citizen of Harpers Ferry, Virginia, one hundred years ago, you would have been proud of its United States Arsenal and Armory, where military rifles were made and stored; and probably you would have felt a little safer for it, because an armory reminded you that your country could protect you. Perhaps you would have been even more proud

3

of the beauty of your quiet little town where nothing much ever happened. Around it rose tall hills, and beneath these flowed two clear, swift rivers, the Potomac and the Shenandoah, to join here and continue on eastward to Washington, the nation's capital, not many miles to the east.

But one October day in 1859, Harpers Ferry, with its armory and arsenal that had made you feel so secure, turned into a fearful place. Inside the arsenal crouched armed invaders who had entered Harpers Ferry at night and seized the Army's buildings. These desperate men had taken thirteen prisoners and held them now as hostages. Among them was George Washington's great-nephew, Colonel Lewis Washington. The invaders had sent out raiding parties to free the slaves in the surrounding countryside and to call on all the Negroes of Virginia to

4

The raiders were led by a giant, gray-bearded old man

rise against their masters. They were led by a giant, gray-bearded old man.

And so in Harpers Ferry there echoed the shots of angry riflemen, and dead men lay in the streets, citizens and raiders alike. The slaves did not rise, but the people did not breathe more easily until they learned that regular troops were on the way to reinforce the young militiamen and townsmen who now surrounded and besieged the arsenal and armory. Most of the raiders inside were wounded or dead, but the men and women and children of Harpers Ferry and Virginia did not know what horror the invaders might have already unloosed. What if Virginia's slaves should rise as had Nat Turner nearly thirty years before to shed blood throughout the South? Hanging, said the people of Harpers Ferry, was too good for the men inside the arsenal who had murdered innocent men and had violated the laws of the United States and the peace and dignity of the sovereign state of Virginia.

The regular troops did not reach the frightened town until long after dark that night of October 17th. The first reinforcements to arrive were United States Marines, who had been rushed by train from Baltimore. They had been followed by a tall, dark-haired and black-mustached lieutenant colonel of the United States Army, who looked much younger than his fifty-two years and who took command of them. That morning he had been ordered by the War Department in Washington to put down some strange insurrection in Harpers Ferry. With him now was a young Army lieutenant and the lieutenant of Marines. Together they stood in the midnight dark inside the armory grounds, surveying the engine house from which the surviving raiders fired now and then in defiance.

The troops should wait until dawn, the colonel decided, before storming the engine house. To attack now might bring injury or death to the hostages inside. And so at dawn the young Army lieutenant walked under a white flag to the engine house and delivered a written demand for surrender to the tall, bearded man who opened the door, a carbine in his hand.

"If they refuse," the colonel had told the lieutenant, "don't talk with them any further. Jump aside and signal. The Marines will then attack." And to the Marine lieutenant in charge of the detachment he said, "Pick twelve men for a storming party. When the lieutenant signals with his hat, go take those men out."

It was seven o'clock in the morning.

In the misty haze, the colonel watched the brief conference at the engine house only forty feet away. Suddenly the lieutenant jumped aside, waved his hat, and shouted, "Come on!" The Marines charged at the double. From the engine house spat rifle fire. Two marines fell, one dead and the other wounded. The rest battered at the door with a long ladder. It

8

The marines battered at the door with a long ladder

splintered and the Marines stormed inside.

In a matter of seconds the fighting was over. Four dead marauders lay on the floor and another was dying. Their gaunt leader was bleeding from sword wounds. The thirteen hostages, citizens of Harpers Ferry and the countryside around, were conducted outside. After them followed the band's wounded leader and two uninjured men. The rest of the twenty-two who had crept into Harpers Ferry two nights before were either dead or too badly wounded to walk.

"Treat the wounded," the colonel ordered, "and hold all the prisoners for the civil authorities." Then he turned aside to write a report for the Secretary of War concerning the uprising which he would later describe as a cruel and senseless deed inspired by a madman.

The desperados, he noted, had been led by

a man of whom he had heard before, a killer from Kansas. This man had raged through the western territories as a fighting Abolitionist who would use any means, including slaying, to free a slave or punish a slaveholder. The man's name, the colonel noted in his report, was John Brown. Ossawattomie John Brown was what they called him out west in Kansas.

The colonel signed his name to the report: Robert E. Lee, Lieutenant Colonel, U.S.A.

Then, his eyes troubled, and his handsome face tense with indignation, Colonel Lee ordered the lieutenant to lead a searching party into Maryland to round up any others of the band who might be lingering and to capture the guns and pikes that John Brown had stored in Maryland to arm the slaves.

Not long afterward the divided and warring American nation would ring with the names of

John Brown, the hater of slavery and man of violence who dedicated himself to freeing slaves; and of Robert E. Lee of Virginia who likewise hated slavery and, in 1862, freed his own slaves, but who followed the road of honor at his conscience's order into the valley of defeat and on to immortality. They would hear, too, of the young Army lieutenant who would become a general of cavalry under Virginia's Lee. His name was J. E. B. Stuart. But none of these three could have known all this on the crisp October day in 1859; neither the anti-slavery zealot who would die two months later on the gallows, nor the colonel who captured him and would himself be a captive six years later of the nation he now served; nor the young lieutenant who would fail his commander at a place named Gettysburg, when he was most needed. And neither John Brown nor Robert

E. Lee could have dreamed on this fateful day that they would be ennobled in history and in legend, the one as a symbol of a man's abhorrence of slavery, and the other a symbol of honor and high courage that could triumph over all defeat.

This is the story of Robert E. Lee, a soldier more loved in defeat than most leaders have ever been in victory.

The story did not begin in Harpers Ferry that autumn evening. Nor did Colonel Robert E. Lee know that his years of tragic greatness lay ahead. Perhaps he saw at Harpers Ferry, as we can see now, the dreadful outlines of the conflict that was to come. But he did not think a civil war was inevitable. And it need not have come at all had not the South, and the North too, listened to stubborn, angry men instead of to leaders who counseled peace and compromise. They did not heed the quieter voices, and war came.

Out of this war of brothers also came lasting unity and traditions by which we Americans live today. None of these shines more brightly than the tradition of honor and duty that Robert E. Lee left to the defeated men and women of the Confederacy as they turned to the hard task of building from the ashes.

2

The Son of Light-Horse Harry

In the early days of the American colonies and even after our Revolution, the principal families of Virginia were the nearest to nobility that a republic could produce. The boy who was born in a magnificent manor on the Potomac, named Stratford, in January, 1807, and christened Robert Edward, was doubly a member of this select group. His father, whom the

Revolutionary War veterans lovingly remembered as Light-Horse Harry Lee, was a hero of our war for freedom. As young General Henry Lee, he had been privileged to enjoy the friendship and confidence of the great George Washington himself.

Of the Lees of Virginia, our first President said that he knew of no country in which a family had contributed so much to its welfare as had the Lees to America.

Early in the 17th century Richard Lee became one of Virginia's earliest leaders. His son, Thomas, built Stratford, the family mansion on the Potomac, and it was there that Robert Edward was born.

And if it was a proud blessing to be born a Lee, it was just as prideful to be a Carter, and Robert Edward Lee's mother was Ann Hill Carter, the daughter of Charles Carter whose mansion, Shirley, was the stateliest in Virginia, and a granddaughter of old Robert "King" Carter, the richest and most notable of the early Virginians.

To be a Lee and a Carter—or one of their kinsmen like the Fitzhughs and Randolphs and Peytons and other blue-blooded folk— meant more than just being a member of a closely knit group of interrelated, aristocratic families, most of them born to a tradition of wealth and leadership. These Virginians were given something else to be proud of that was much more meaningful. It was a tradition of honor that demanded a high standard of personal behavior, good citizenship, a willingness for public service, a sense of obligation to the less fortunate, a deep, fierce loyalty to family and to state, and a firm belief in the goodness and wisdom of God. We want to remember especially this feeling of loyalty to the state, for it was to become the most decisive fact in the life of Robert E. Lee.

The French have a phrase for this tradition. *Noblesse oblige,* they say, which means that the wellborn have an obligation to do the right thing always. To these Virginians honor was the most important thing in life.

It was just as well that being a Lee and a Carter meant more than being simply the owner of vast lands and scores of slaves and a house with a huge ballroom. For while young Robert E. Lee was born to such luxuries, he never enjoyed them in his boyhood and young manhood. Instead, it was his lot to be a poor relation, and this condition and the reason for it were also greatly significant in shaping his life. The Lee family's money difficulties were the fault of his hero father. Had it not been for the small financial resources of his devoted mother, Robert would have been an even poorer relation than he was. This near-poverty helped him to decide on a military career, for it was partly because of lack of funds for a private college education that he entered West Point and so became a soldier like his father before him.

Most of us would have been as dazzled by that father as were the Lee family and his fellow Virginians. Light-Horse Harry's deeds of daring in the Revolution were legendary even before the war for our freedom was over. Time and again he defeated the British by his brilliant maneuvering; and Congress had given him a special gold medal for his military services. He had fought side by side with South Carolina's Marion, the Swamp Fox, and Sumter, the guerrilla. The noble Marquis de Lafayette, who had come from France to fight for American freedom, cherished this young man. It was Light-Horse Harry Lee, always worshiping his old commander, who had written

Light-Horse Harry Lee was given a special gold medal

and declaimed at Washington's funeral the enduring description of our first President as being also "first in war, first in peace and first in the hearts of his countrymen."

In Henry Lee's young manhood he was as wealthy as he was heroic. So great was his fame and popularity after the Revolution that he served as Virginia's governor. His first wife had been a cousin, Matilda Lee, who was mistress of the great plantation, Stratford. Before she died in 1790, she had borne him four children. Then he married Ann Carter, seventeen years younger than he, to her father's great concern; for there was another side to this man, and young Ann must have known of it though she was willing in her love to overlook it.

The unpleasant truth was that Light-Horse Harry was not a man for peacetime or for business. He wanted to amass great wealth and he tried many schemes, often foolish and always unsuccessful ones, to achieve his ambition. But all he did was lose everything he had, lands and farms and money; and—far worse to a Lee—the speculations injured some of his friends and his own reputation. Robert Edward was next to the youngest of the four boys and two girls who came to the second union. Finally when Robert was only two years old, his father was clapped into debtor's prison for a year by his creditors. This was a curious and useless punishment of those days for unfortunate or careless persons who could not pay their debts. This treatment of his adored father, and Light-Horse Harry's bad record as a money manager, made an early and lasting impression on Robert, no less than on the mother who taught him the virtues—thrift and self-denial—his father lacked. Never would he be found lax in any matter relating to money, either his own or other people's.

The experience of being jailed must have badly hurt the proud and aging Light-Horse Harry. Moreover, he and his family could no longer stay at Stratford, for that beautiful home had been the estate of his dead first wife. In 1810 it came into the possession of their oldest son, Henry, now a man. So, tired and angry and still dreaming foolish dreams of financial success, Light-Horse Harry took his family to the little city of Alexandria, Virginia, just across the Potomac River from Washington. There they settled in a small, pleasant brick house on Cameron Street that could hold only a few of the lovely pieces of furniture from Stratford. What money they had to live on came almost entirely from the small dowry which Ann Carter's father had given her, and which she would

He took his family to the little city of Alexandria

watch carefully so that her children in later years could be housed and clothed and fed and educated.

But Light-Horse Harry had not suffered all

that he would. In 1812, war again broke out between England and the United States. A good many Americans believed that this new struggle was unnecessary and that it had been brought about by war-hungry men. Light-Horse Harry, the old fighter, was among those who protested against the new conflict. Another critic of the war was Alexander Hanson, son of an old friend and editor of *The Federal Republican* in Baltimore, who had denounced it with great vigor in his newspaper. A pro-war mob had already destroyed his building and all his printing equipment because of his outspoken opposition. Lee had written Hanson words of encouragement and had given instructions on how to barricade his new quarters against attackers. Hanson soon printed another issue of his newspaper, and this increased the anger of his enemies.

The day the new issue appeared, Light-Horse Harry Lee was visiting in Baltimore. He sensed that Hanson was in danger and rushed to join him and a handful of others in the house which the editor was now using as residence and temporary office. Among this handful was John Howard Payne, who later wrote the song "Home, Sweet Home."

Outside a mob began gathering in the street. Light-Horse Harry, the light of battle in his eyes, directed the barricading of the house and gave the defenders a quick lesson in how to hold off an enemy. In a little while members of the mob commenced firing. When the defenders returned the fire, one of the attackers was killed and another one wounded. Then, just before the howling mob could storm the house, the city militia arrived and Lee, Hanson and their friends, twenty-three in all, agreed to surrender. That was the morning of July 28, 1812. Hanson and his friends were taken to the city jail and placed together in a large cell for safekeeping. Disgracefully, the authorities took no notice of their assailants.

That night the berserk mob swarmed into the almost unprotected jail. Not enough troops had been kept in readiness to protect the Hanson group. A few of the prisoners broke loose. Of those who fell into the rioters' hands, one was killed and eight others were terribly beaten and slashed by the drunken avengers. One of these victims was Light-Horse Harry Lee. His tormentors, trying to see if he was dead or only unconscious, dropped hot candle grease in his eyes and tried to cut off his nose, then left him for dead, with his face terribly gashed.

The hardy old Revolutionary lived, but he was crippled and disfigured and unable to work for the rest of his days. He determined to leave his country for a while in search of health and to forget the past. And so he did, a year after the cowardly attack in Baltimore, bidding good-bye to the devoted family he would never see again. He died some five years later after falling ill on the ship which was bringing him home.

Little Robert was only six when his father left, but he must have remembered until the end of his days the family's heartaches when his father left the little house in Alexandria. He could not have known then that the departure of his father meant that he would in time be nurse and housekeeper for his ailing mother.

Sidney, the first-born, had died when only a year old. Charles, the oldest surviving son, was fourteen when his father sailed away. Sister Ann was thirteen and never well, and Smith

28

was ten. Robert, only a little older than the baby sister, Catherine Mildred, soon became nurse and housekeeper for his ailing mother. Circumstances caused him to take on responsibilities far beyond his years. Honor and duty directed him to perform tasks which most boys would neglect or mock because they thought them to be women's work. But there was nothing womanish about young Robert. He was all boy, vigorous and fun-loving; his heavy and unusual duties at home helped build the character of the man he was to become.

3

A Boy in Alexandria

Although we do not always realize it, we are greatly shaped by the events and the surroundings and even the ideas that we experience when we are very young. And so the childhood and older boyhood days of Robert E. Lee helped to determine his character as a man.

The most lasting influence in his life was his brave, sick mother. Because of her husband's folly in money matters she preached to her youngest son thrift and wisdom and honor in money dealings, economy in his personal life and a willingness to give up or not look for luxuries that he couldn't afford. He could say years later, in all truth, that he owed everything that he was to his mother.

He had a hero-worshiping admiration, too, for his father. No one reminded him of his father's weaknesses and he never mentioned them himself. But there were reminders everywhere of his father's courage—in the stories his mother told, in the yarns spun by the veterans of Lee's Legion who lived in Alexandria, and in the loving boasts of his many cousins. They were proud of Light-Horse Harry, no matter how dismally his life had ended.

In the years before his death, the old warrior had continued to write to his family even from such a distance. Some of the advice he gave his sons would have greatly helped Light-Horse Harry Lee himself had he followed it long before.

These are some of the things that he told one of his sons:

"I would rather see you unlettered and unnoticed, if virtuous in practice as well as theory, than to see you the equal in glory to the great Washington."

"Fame in arms or art is nothing unless bottomed on virtue."

"Self command is a pivot upon which the character of fame and independence of us mortals hang."

"Cleanliness of person is not only comely to all beholders but is indispensable to sanctity of body. Trained by the best of mothers to value it, you will never lose sight of it."

"You know my abhorrence of lying and you have often been told by me that it led to every vice and cancelled every tendency to virtue. Never forget this truth and disdain this mean and infamous practice."

"Avoid debt, the sink of mental power and the subversion of independence, which draws into debasement every virtue, in appearance certaintly if not in reality."

Just as influential as the devotion of his mother and the patriotic record of his father in shaping young Robert's character was the inspiration of the dead George Washington. From the time he could understand, he had heard his father and his mother speak of Washington in almost religious reverence. Everywhere in Alexandria were reminders of this greatest of all Americans. From there Washington, in his young manhood, had led his

As a child, Robert had heard his father speak of the dead George Washington in almost religious reverence

Rangers to fight beside the doomed English General Braddock in the French and Indian War. Here he had established Revolutionary headquarters, and close by was his stately home Mount Vernon. The history of the American colonies and the young United States filled the town of Alexandria. And, wonder of wonders, before young Robert was out of his teens the venerable Marquis de Lafayette, the dear comrade of Washington, voyaged from France as an old and honored friend to visit in the home of the widow of Light-Horse Harry Lee and shake the hand of her son. The military tradition must have begun to run strong in young Robert's blood from his earliest days. It was almost inevitable that he should try to model his behavior by what he knew and read and heard of George Washington.

Together with his youthful pride in his family, his country and its leaders and his hero father, he had a loving pride in Virginia. It is difficult for us today to understand how a state could mean as much as and even more than the United States itself. But we must remember that these first thirteen states of the young nation had been separate colonies not long before Robert E. Lee's birth, each with a conviction of its independence from the others. They had rebelled as colonies, not as the United States. The idea of a single nation, closely and forever bound, did not then appeal to every American.

Among the original colonies none had a more glorious past and none a more decisive part in creating the young Republic of the United States than had Virginia. Virginia had given Washington and Jefferson and Patrick Henry and Madison and many another soldier and statesman to the country. Her leaders ranked high in the nation's councils. Her present, like her past, was brilliant, and her people loved intensely her fragrant meadows and rich, green fields and blue-green mountains. To be a Virginian, they said and believed, was to live among the happiest and the worthiest people in all the world. Virginia had given them everything they had. They would fight anybody and everybody if she were threatened, as the British had threatened her during the Revolution and again during the War of 1812 when they burned nearby Washington and made Alexandria itself pay a ransom to escape a like fate. Seven-year-old Robert E. Lee had even seen the smoke rising from the capital of his country that black day in 1814 when the British landed and burned the White House itself.

And, lastly, Robert E. Lee, the man, was

shaped by the responsibilities which Robert, the boy, assumed at an age when most youngsters worried only over their studies and what games to play next. By this time his mother was gradually becoming an invalid. Before Robert was twelve he was practically running the house, making the purchases, learning how to shop wisely, to hand out the food supplies to the servants and to do the hundred and one tasks that mothers usually perform.

Perhaps it was because of this self-discipline that he never drank or smoked in his life. At any rate, the care of his mother and the supervision of the household were the principal duties of his boyhood. But this does not mean that his youth was unhappy or that he had no fun. The Lees were poor only by comparison with their relatives. They had enough to live comfortably. And Robert also had time for play

Robert also had time to go hunting with his friends

and for study. He played and hunted and swam
in the Potomac with his Alexandria playmates;
he learned to ride; and he looked forward to
the visits to the plantation homes of his cousins
as much as they looked forward to his coming,

for he was tall and strong and athletic and excelled in outdoor games.

He got most of his early schooling at the Alexandria Academy, which in 1821 was made free to all boys who lived in Alexandria. His principal teacher was an able Irishman named William B. O'Leary, and for three years he studied Greek and Latin and mathematics, doing especially well in algebra and geometry. Another of his teachers, under whom he completed his Alexandria school years, gave a description of Robert's best talent.

"He is good at finishing up," Benjamin Hallowell said.

The three years he attended the Alexandria Academy gave him almost all the formal schooling he had in his boyhood. Before then he had been taught at home. Afterward he would enter the Military Academy. By the time he was seventeen he had taken all the courses that Mr. O'Leary could offer. The natural question rose: What should he do next? Some Lees and Carters had left the plantations for the ministry, for medicine, for law, for politics, even for business careers. But the Lee who mattered most to young Robert, his father, had been a soldier. If he could enter West Point, his mother would not have to pay for his schooling from her small income; and best of all, Robert, like his father before him, could wear his country's uniform.

4

A Cadet at West Point

Back in the 1820s the entrance requirements for West Point were not nearly as strict as they are now. Still it was not easy to become an Army cadet because many more boys wanted to enter the Army than the Academy could hold; and that remains true today.

The candidate had to be between fourteen and twenty years old, at least four feet nine inches in height—not very tall—and without any physical handicaps. He had to be able to read and write well and was expected to be good in arithmetic. He must agree to stay in the Army five years, including the four years as a cadet. At least one thousand young Americans of Robert E. Lee's day sought appointments, but only 250 cadets could be trained at a time. The applicants were appointed by the President under the nomination of the Secretary of War. As with everything else, the influence of good citizens counted.

Ann Carter Lee must have been proud of the enthusiasm with which the kinsmen and friends of her dead husband and the members of her own family supported her son's application. William H. Fitzhugh, a longtime, loyal counselor of the family, gave him a personal letter of introduction to the Secretary of War,

John C. Calhoun, praising Robert's dead father and his mother; and describing him in glowing terms:

Ravensworth Feb 7th 1824.

My dear Sir,

I cannot permit the young gentleman, who will hand you this letter, to make his intended application, without carrying with him, such testimony in his behalf, as a long & an intimate acquaintance both with himself and his family, justify me in giving. He is the son of Gen. Henry Lee, with whose history, you are, of course, acquainted; and who (whatever may have been the misfortune of his latter years) had certainly established, by his revolutionary services, a strong claim to the gratitude

44

of his country. He is the son also of one of the finest women, the State of Virginia has ever produced. Possessed, in a very eminent degree, of all those qualities, which peculiarly belong to the female character of the South, she is rendered doubly interesting by her meritorious & successful exertions to support, in comfort, a large family, and to give to all her children excellent educations.

The young gentleman, whom I have now the pleasure of introducing to you, as a candidate for West-point, is her youngest son. An intimate acquaintance, & a constant intercourse with him, almost from his infancy, authorize me to speak in the most unqualified terms of his amiable disposition, & his correct and gentlemanly habits. He is disposed to devote himself to the profession of arms. But his final determination on this subject, must, of course, depend on the result of his present application, and you will find him prepared to acquiesce in whatever decision, circumstances may require you to make in his case. Next, however, to promising him the commission, which he asks, the greatest favor you can do him will be to tell him promptly if you think the obstacles to his success are insurmountable. His own age (eighteen I believe) and the situation of his mother require that he should lose no time in selecting the employment to which his future life is to be devoted.

Accept my dear Sir the assurance of

the very great respect with which

I am

Yo^r &c

W. H. Fitzhugh

Robert handed it personally to Secretary Calhoun. His teachers, his older brothers and many senators and congressmen joined in sponsoring him.

In March, 1824, Robert was notified that he was accepted; but because of the large number of prospective cadets, he was told that he could not enter the Academy until July, 1825. Immediately, he accepted the appointment. Here are the letters that he and his mother wrote. In his excitement he misspelled "honored."

Sir

I hereby accept the appointment to the station of a Cadet in the service of the United States, with which I have been honnoured by the President.

The above is the declaration of consent which my letter of appointment instructs me should accompany my acceptance.

I remain with the highest respect, Sir

Your most obliged & most obedient Servant

R. E. Lee

Alex^a. April 1st 1824

To

The Honble J. C. Calhoun

Sir

As the surviving Parent of Robert E.

Lee I consent to his signing articles, binding himself to serve as a Cadet five years, to be computed from the time of his joining the Military Academy.

Ann H. Lee

More than a year later, in June, 1825, a tall, sturdy and unusually handsome young man of eighteen traveled by stagecoach and river steamer to the young republic's Military Academy at West Point, thirty-seven miles up-river from New York, where the few drab military buildings were as uninspiring as the scenery against which they rose was beautiful. West Point was then only twenty-three years old. Two dormitories, a two-story academic building and a mess hall were all that had been erected for the use and instruction of the cadets. The food was unbelievably bad and the discipline was stern. A cadet was forbidden to play cards or drink or smoke. His bare quarters must be free of any novels or games. He could go nowhere beyond the limits of the Academy without permission, not even to bathe in the Hudson River. Fist fights could mean expulsion and so could hazing. One upperclassman, a cadet named Jefferson Davis whom Lee would know exceedingly well in later years, almost was expelled for violating the out-of-bound rules. He was found guilty but his good record earned him leniency, and he remained at the Academy.

For his personal toilet the cadet could have in his room—which he shared with three others —only a looking glass, a pitcher, a tin pail, a broom, a washstand and basin, and a scrubbing brush. The bugle sounded reveille at dawn, and the cadets were studying mathematics on an

Every cadet took part in dress parade at West Point

empty stomach before seven o'clock. Then followed parade and classes of study and military exercise with only a scant hour of free time after midday dinner. And after dress parade and roll call and supper, the student must retire to his room and study until 9:30 when tatoo sounded, followed by another roll call, with lights out by ten o'clock.

But this kind of life did not seem as bad to Robert and his fellow cadets as it does now to us. A soldier's life, they knew, was no bed of roses, and they had voluntarily sought it. Neither officers nor men had the luxuries or even the necessities that we are accustomed to today.

Upon arrival, Robert appeared before the academic board for the oral examination that would determine for each appointee whether he could remain at West Point. A few days later, the expectant candidates formed ranks in front of the barracks. As they stood at attention, an instructor told them that the names of the successful candidates would be read off. Those fortunate ones would step forward four paces as their names were called.

A few moments later Cadet Robert E. Lee advanced four paces. The day was June 28, 1825. Within the hour he had bought the required equipment for his barracks room and his military clothing—an impressive gray uniform, some white trousers, a blue fatigue jacket and a high, black leather parade cap decorated with a yellow metal design and with a black plume for dress occasions and a less formal leather cockade for all other times. To his delight he wore his dress uniform for the first time when the cadet corps paraded a few weeks later in honor of the visiting Marquis de Lafayette.

From the very first day the young Virginian stood out in his studies, in military conduct and in general behavior. His strong body enabled him to withstand the hardships of cadet training. He was particularly apt in engineering, the Academy's most difficult course. He was every inch a soldier; and when he was graduated four years later, he had made a remarkable record. Never had he received a demerit for any bad behavior or for breaking of the rules. Upon graduation he stood second in his class of forty-six, the survivors of eighty-seven hopefuls. He was cadet officer of his class and won the highest military distinction that could be given to any student, that of being appointed adjutant of the corps.

This is what his close friend and classmate, Joseph E. Johnston, who would become one of his most trusted generals in the Civil War, said of him in later years:

"We had the same intimate associates who thought as I did that no other youth or man so united the qualities that win warm friendship and command high respect. For he was full of sympathy and kindness, genial and fond of gay conversation and of fun; while his correctness of demeanor and attention to all duties, personal and official, and a dignity as much a part of himself as the elegance of his person, gave him a superiority that everyone acknowledged in his heart. He was the only one of all the men I have known who could laugh at the faults and follies of his friends in such a manner as to make them ashamed without touching their affection for him, and to confirm their respect and sense of his superiority."

That is as rare a tribute as any man could receive, and especially a young man.

By now Robert E. Lee was nearly six feet tall, of athletic build and possessing a mature dignity. Robert did not come home until he had completed his first two years at the Academy. Expenses and the disciplinary life prevented him. It was on this furlough that he discovered that a slim, blonde, nineteen-year-old girl whom he had known almost all his life seemed enchantingly different now from the way he had remembered her. Her name was Mary Custis. She was the daughter of a proud gentleman, George Washington Park Custis, who was President Washington's adopted son and the grandson of Washington's wife, Martha. The Custises lived at Arlington, a high-columned hilltop home, overlooking the Potomac near Washington. Mary had been born there. As a young boy, Robert had played frequently with Mary when he had visited the Custises with his mother and sister. But then they had been children. Now a gray-uniformed cadet and a lovely Virginia girl found that an old friendship had grown into something more. Together they entered upon the summer's round of parties; and before Robert returned to West Point he had won Mary's promise to marry him after he was graduated from the Academy.

Mary Custis was the apple of her father's eye, a gay young woman, indulged in her every wish by her doting father and as light-hearted as Robert was serious. Old Mr. Custis hadn't liked the idea of penniless young Robert E. Lee taking his daughter as a bride. He didn't see much future in being a soldier. But Mary Ann had one ally worth all others together. That was her mother who was delighted with the son of Light-Horse Harry.

The wedding had to wait until Robert was graduated, at the very least, and that was not until the Fourth of July, 1829. Immediately the young second lieutenant went into the Army

Robert won lovely Mary Custis' promise to marry him

Corps of Engineers. But his happiness at his approaching marriage and his success at West Point were marred that summer by the illness and death of his long-suffering mother. Robert spent his first week after coming home in constant attendance upon her, and he was at her bedside when she died within a month after his graduation.

Back on duty with the Army Engineers, Second Lieutenant Lee was engaged in a variety of duties. First he was sent to Savannah, Georgia, to construct a fort at nearby Cockspur Island, and to keep the sea waters from flooding it. From the obscure Georgia fort, where he labored daily in water up to his shoulders, he was sent to larger Fortress Monroe, across Hampton Roads from Norfolk, Virginia, to work upon the fortifications. From there he went back to Arlington to marry Mary Ann Custis. It was in June, 1831, nearly two years after his graduation, that Robert and Mary were married at Arlington, a glowing event that brought together the first families of Virginia to witness the wedding of a Custis and a Lee. After their wedding the lieutenant and his bride returned to Fortress Monroe.

From now on Arlington, residence of his father-in-law and hallowed by many relics of George Washington, would be Robert E. Lee's home too. There would his happiest years be spent. And already the old hands in the Army, the generals and colonels, were predicting a brilliant future for the son of Light-Horse Harry.

5

A Soldier's Business Is War

Few really great soldiers have ever preferred war to peace. But a soldier's business is fighting, and when there is no war, time can hang heavy on his hands.

Robert E. Lee must have found military life dull for most of his first fifteen years in the Army. But his happy family life at Arlington helped make up for it. His married life was blessed with a rare devotion between him and Mary Custis Lee.

Seven children were born to the Lees in fourteen years: a son, George Washington Custis Lee, a daughter Mary, another son William Fitzhugh, whom his father called Rooney, and four more: Agnes, Annie, Robert Edward and Mildred.

Nevertheless, as a soldier there was not much to interest him in those peaceful years between his graduation from West Point in 1829 and the year 1845. Sometimes he performed military office work in Washington; he served as an engineering officer in the Midwest and again at Fortress Monroe, and built coastal defenses with inadequate funds because, as always, Congress was unwilling to spend much money on the Army in peacetime.

Only once in those fifteen years was he given

a truly vital task. That was in St. Louis, already a promising Mississippi River port city. It was in danger of being blocked from the tawny father of waters by massive islands of silt. The Missouri River, flowing into the Mississippi a little to the north of the growing city, had deposited these along the St. Louis side while cutting a deep channel on the Illinois side to the east. If this process kept up, the newly formed islands would seal off the harbor of St. Louis; and without a river harbor, the city would have little reason for existence.

Because the United States Engineers were then, as now, responsible for keeping the nation's rivers navigable, Captain Lee was sent to St. Louis to do what he could. His commanding general, Winfield Scott, said: "Lee is young, but if the work can be done, he can do it."

Lee worked out a brilliant plan. Far into the

river across from the Illinois side to the most
northerly of the silt islands above St. Louis,
he built a great dike. When the Missouri's down-
ward rushing current struck this dike, it veered
toward the St. Louis side, and in time washed
away the islands that threatened to doom the
city. It was not so easy as it may seem. Captain
Lee took three years to finish the dike, but they
were good years. His wife and children enjoyed
the exciting West with him; he was performing
a worth-while mission, and he had the great
satisfaction of meeting his first big test.

Five years later Robert E. Lee, a captain
still because promotions come slowly in a peacetime army, was stationed at Fort Hamilton in
New York. A soldier all his mature life, he had
never heard a shot fired in combat. Now his
country had declared war on smaller Mexico.

The rights and wrongs of that war are still

64

debated and certainly many Americans of that day, including Abraham Lincoln, believed that the United States was wrong to fight her small Southern neighbor. The United States and Mexico had fallen out over their common boundary, the Rio Grande River, which had been set up when the Republic of Texas came into the Union. The Texans had seceded from Mexico in 1836, proclaimed their independence, and defeated the Mexicans in a no-quarter struggle. In 1845, the United States annexed the delighted Texans; and when a band of Mexican soldiers crossed the Rio Grande a year later, President Polk announced that a state of war existed.

To a soldier the declaration of war meant action and a chance to fight for his country. Impatiently Captain Lee waited for more than three months for his orders. Fellow officers, including Jefferson Davis, had struck southward under tough General Zachary Taylor across the Rio Grande and were fighting and winning battles on Mexican soil—at Palo Alto and Resaca de la Palma and Monterey—against one-legged Santa Anna, the soldier-president of Mexico. Finally Lee was ordered to join the American forces stationed at San Antonio.

"At last," he said, "action at last." But he was to be disappointed for a while yet. Because of his talent as an engineer he was assigned to build roads in northern Mexico. Occasionally he led scouting parties through the countryside looking for Santa Anna's men, but he didn't see sight or sound of an enemy.

Then President Polk decided to match the southward thrust with an attack from the sea. He planned a campaign which would begin at Vera Cruz, on the eastern coast of Mexico, and end with the capture of Mexico City, the capital.

The Americans built up a powerful armada at Brazos where the Rio Grande enters the Gulf of Mexico. The nation's foremost military hero, old General Scott, commanded the expedition, and the brilliant Captain Lee, who had never faced an enemy in all his thirty-nine years, was assigned to Scott's forces. An engineer, skilled in building roads and bridges and in erecting fortifications, is a valuable man for an invading army. Now Captain Lee's peacetime reputation would be tested in war.

On his horse, Creole, Captain Lee rode across southeastern Texas to the port of Brazos. The brother officers he met there included many who would win fame in later years, fighting beside him in the Confederate Army or seeking to destroy him in battle: his dear friend Joe Johnston,

Albert Sidney Johnston, Pierre G. T. Beauregard, Stonewall Jackson, George Pickett, A. P. Hill and Jubal Early, all of whom would serve as generals in the Confederate armies; and U. S. Grant, George McClellan, Irvin McDowell and a half dozen others who would lead Union forces against them.

On March 3rd the fleet sailed with the Army which would make the nation's first assault upon an enemy from the sea. A few days later Lee came under fire for the first time in his life. Off Vera Cruz, General Scott and a group of his staff officers, the Virginia captain among them, skirted the shore in a small boat. The Mexicans opened fire, but luckily their aim was poor. No one was hit.

Three weeks later Vera Cruz had fallen. In its capture Captain Lee had played a major part, for he had selected the location for the

68

naval siege guns and supervised the building of the attackers' redoubts. Writing home, he penned words not ordinarily expected from a soldier: "My heart bled for the inhabitants. It was awful. The soldiers I did not care so much for, but it was terrible to think of the women and the children."

Soon after Vera Cruz fell, the American army pushed inland toward Mexico City. Lee and his engineers rode and walked and climbed, always in the lead, setting and breaking the trail across rivers and mountains, seeking out the foe. At Cerro Gordo, a ranch dominating a mountain pass, Santa Anna made his first stand, in a position that seemed to defy storming. Again General Scott called upon his captain of engineers. "Find a way to attack the enemy from the rear," he ordered.

It was the most dangerous task Robert E.

Lee had undertaken. He found himself behind enemy lines, creeping through cactus and in the ravines and stony outcroppings. Always he was in danger of discovery as he studied the ground for a vantage point. Once as he knelt beside a spring to get a cooling drink of water, he heard Mexican soldiers chattering near by. Quickly he plunged behind a log, concealing himself with underbrush. A Mexican mounted the log but didn't see the hidden American. He sat down on it and was joined by another. Not until night could Lee make his way back to the American lines; but the next day he and his engineers cut a road to the place he had chosen behind the Mexican lines.

The battle of Cerro Gordo was fought on April 17th and 18th. Two columns of Americans attacked the Mexicans from the front and the third struck from the rear, where Lee guided

The Mexican soldiers didn't see the hidden American

the attack on both days. The Mexicans counted their dead and wounded and captured in many hundreds. "You have no idea what a horrible sight a field of battle is," Lee wrote his son Custis.

It was not captain but Major Lee, newly promoted in the field and praised by General Scott for his bearing and endurance, who set out early in August, again in the Army's van, for Mexico City.

When the Americans reached the almost impregnable capital of Mexico, it was Robert E. Lee upon whom General Scott called to scout the swamps and lakes and rocky fields of lava for a way to attack the enemy from the rear.

In the next thirty-six hours of the battle for Mexico City, Major Lee displayed courage, military genius and physical endurance that almost defy belief. It was as if he had known from boyhood that a lifetime of clean living, without indulgence in tobacco and drink, was necessary to fit him for this supreme effort for his country. With some infantry and dragoons, he set out first to discover among the lava beds the best approaches to the capital. No sooner had that difficult scouting mission been accomplished than he guided another advance unit to the Mexican rear. Their first objective was a village where Mexican outposts waited to harass the attackers. These had to be cleared out. Across a five-mile field of lava that could rip a man's shoes and skin to shreds, Lee led the blue-clad Americans. The lava field was called the Pedregal, and it was beyond this treacherous field that the enemy waited.

The Mexicans discovered the approaching Americans early, and additional Mexican forces began to try to surround them. This time it was the Americans who were in danger of being attacked from behind and overwhelmed. The commanding officer of the column, General Persifor Smith, decided to send for reinforcements, and notify General Scott to attack the village from all sides before the Mexicans behind him could put the same plan in effect. "I will go back to headquarters, sir," volunteered Major Lee. In the darkness he set out again with a few men across the dangerous ravine-slitted field in a drenching rain. It was just before midnight when he stumbled into General Scott's tent.

Seven men had tried to go from Scott's force to Lee's party during the day. None had made it. His was the first contact between the two American forces.

Major Lee presented General Smith's re-

Major Lee presented the request for reinforcements

quest for reinforcements and his plan for the
attack. General Scott agreed to it. And almost
unbelievably, back across the Pedregal went
Robert E. Lee to bring the good news to General Smith. The Americans hit the Mexicans
from the rear and frontally, and in less than
half an hour the enemy again was in flight.

Again Lee crossed the treacherous Pedregal to report the victory to General Scott. And again Scott sent the tired Major, who already had traveled twenty wearisome miles, on another trip to find out by what road the army should pursue the fleeing Mexicans.

"Lee's journeys across the Pedregal were the greatest feat of physical and moral courage performed by any individual to my knowledge in the campaign," General Scott reported.

Nothing seemed to halt the Virginian. Finally he led one column across a river protecting the capital to the very walls of the city. Not until then did he rest.

Nor did glory end there. It was Robert E. Lee who advised General Scott to make a direct attack on Chapultepec, most formidable of all the forts in Mexico. It was Lee who placed the artillery's batteries that were to soften up the foe. It was Lee who made ready for the assault and who guided the first American division to the fort. But Major Lee did not enter the fort at the head of the victorious Americans. His task was to keep the commanding general and the army in contact with each other. A bullet gave him a minor wound. The slight injury did not halt him any more than had the fifty straight hours without sleep, spent in preparing the final assault on Chapultepec. But when the fort fell and he set out to discover how to reach the city's very gates, he reeled and lost consciousness. Never before had the hearty soldier fainted.

Mexico City surrendered the next day. Major Lee had recovered enough to be able to watch the American flag being raised over the Mexican capital. Again he was promoted, this time to brevet colonel, and again the dispatches from the battlefield praised the son of Light-Horse Harry.

With the short war over, Colonel Robert E. Lee came home again to Arlington and to fame.

No doubt the people of the United States were telling each other, as they had done before and have since, that there would be no more wars. For more than ten years Robert E. Lee himself may have believed that peace would be lasting. He delighted in rejoining his wife and playing again with the children, whom he liked to have tickle his hands and feet. Once again his life was serene and unexciting. He considered, but turned down, an offer of Cuban revolutionaries to lead an invasion against their island's Spanish masters. He built a fort in Baltimore harbor. He was appointed superintendent of the U.S. Military Academy at West Point, from which he had graduated with such distinction. The new Secretary of War, under whom he served, was Jefferson Davis. Among the cadets at West Point were Lee's eldest son, Custis, and his nephew, Fitzhugh, both of whom were soon to follow him in battle against many of their classmates.

One of Lee's principal concerns at West Point was discipline. In recent years, the cadets had not been ruled as strictly as they might have been, and Lee set about remedying the situation. He was not unforgivingly stern, however, as one story especially proves.

Two cadets became involved in a forbidden fist fight on the parade ground after some horseplay during parade. An instructor discovered the battlers just as one of them, who had whipped the other, walked away. He demanded that the beaten cadet, Archibald Gracie,

Jr., give his own name and the name of his opponent who by then had vanished. The boy gave his own, but refused to reveal the other cadet's identity.

"Ask him if you find him," he said. "I'm no informer."

Gracie was put under arrest. Next day the other cadet, Wharton Green, entered Lee's office.

"I'm the other fellow in that fight, sir," he said. "I think it's hard on Gracie to get the only punishment after getting a licking. I insist on having the same given to me."

"The offense means a heavy penalty," Lee said. Then when Green again insisted that he also be punished, the commandant smiled. "I'll cancel the report and there'll be no penalty. But don't you think brother cadets should live in peace and harmony?"

Years later, Gracie, by then a Confederate brigadier, shielded Lee from enemy bullets on the ramparts of Petersburg where a desperate battle was fought.

It was during his three years as superintendent at West Point that Lee became a member of the Episcopal Church. He had been blessed with deep moral scruples and an abiding confidence in a God always, but he had never joined the church of his fathers. From now on its influence was never to leave him, nor would his faith in Almighty God, no matter how dark the hour.

Only a few years later the hour would be darker for Robert E. Lee and for his loved Virginia than any man could dream in those years of peace that followed his baptism of fire deep in Mexico.

6

In Defense of Virginia

For most of Robert E. Lee's life up to now, and
especially since his young manhood, something
sad and terrible had been happening to the
American people. Great numbers of Northerners and Southerners were coming to hate each
other and to be almost hopelessly divided over
two principal issues. One issue, slavery, was

moral, and the other, states' rights, was political. Too many of the angry brothers refused to listen to the calmer voices on both sides which sought to heal the widening rift and to resolve the quarrel.

For more than two hundred years, the Southern landowners, whose plantations were given over almost entirely to the raising of cotton and such other large-scale crops as tobacco, had been buying and using thousands of slaves brought over from Africa and their American-born slave descendants to perform unskilled labor in the fields and to work in their country and town homes as servants. Actually, a majority of white Southerners never owned a single slave, and many slave owners and non-slave owners in the South were alike opposed to the slave system. But the white Southerners defended the practice as being necessary for the raising of cotton, upon which the South's economic well-being depended.

Some Southerners even used the Bible to excuse the enslavement of the African, pointing to a passage which seemed to say that black men were doomed to be hewers of woods and drawers of water. But very few people in the industrial North, where slaves were not needed, believed there was any justification for slavery. There just were no good arguments for a practice which to civilized man was growing more and more indefensible.

Nevertheless, most Southerners strongly resented the manner of the North's criticism of slavery and especially the attacks from the more violent antislavery spokesmen who called themselves Abolitionists and who painted the Southern slave owners in the worst possible light. One such was John Brown whom Lee captured at Harpers Ferry.

The angry Southerners said that the Northerners were hypocrites, that Northern slave dealers had made money capturing and selling slaves to the South. They said the only reason that slavery was not customary in the North was that the Yankee manufacturers weren't able to use ignorant slaves in their industries.

The struggle over slavery became something worse than name calling. It grew into bloodshed in the new territories such as Kansas where Ossawattomie John Brown and other deadly men on both sides led bands of killers against their foes. Many slavery and antislavery settlers died, and much property was destroyed. Even women and children were murdered by these fanatics, most of whom simply used the slavery issue as an excuse to rob and kill.

The political quarrel was almost as bitter. The North's leaders, by and large, believed in a strong central government. They considered that the states were bound inseparably together and that the federal power should be supreme. Most of the Southerners looked upon the Union as an agreement among and by the states of their own free will. They believed that a state had the right to leave the Union—or secede, as they termed it—if it so desired. Moreover, the South preferred, as it does to some extent today, a less centralized government. They gave the name "States' Rights" to their position, meaning that a state should have the right to determine for itself what to do about most of its problems. Slavery, the Southerners thought, was such a problem. Leave us alone, the South's leaders said, and we will settle the slavery question. The South's principal leaders believed that each new state, as it came into the Union from the territories, should have the right to decide what it would do about slavery.

All this, of course, simplifies a struggle which grew fiercer and fiercer throughout Robert E. Lee's boyhood and manhood, and which would reach its most violent pre-Civil War peak, as we have seen, with the raid on Harpers Ferry by John Brown, and John Brown's capture by Robert E. Lee and his later execution.

It is certain that Colonel Lee of the United States Army was troubled by the bitter division of his countrymen long before he stood in the dawn outside the arsenal at Harpers Ferry. He was himself torn by conflicting feelings. He was a Southerner, a Lee of Virginia, whose father and kinsmen had contributed so mightily to the making of the American nation. He was an officer in the Army of the United States and one

87

of its heroes. He had been taught from text-
books and by the Virginians he respected that
a state had a free choice of staying in or quitting
the Union. Through his wife he had been a
slaveholder like almost every man of considerable property and wealth in the South. But he
had freed the Custis slaves as his father-in-law
wished, and he was outspoken in his belief that
slavery ruined the slave and the owner alike.
His great heroes, Washington, after whom he
modeled himself, and many another, were Virginians. It is not so easy for us to understand
today how a man might think first of his state
and second of his country. But the nation was
young and the fathers of many of the men who
led it at the eve of the Civil War in 1860 could
remember the colonies to which their own fathers had given first allegiance. This was especially true of the deep-rooted men of the soil,

the South's planters and small farmers whose dear and little world lay within the bounds of the states that they loved and seldom quitted.

But if Robert E. Lee's heart was troubled, his military career and family life had been almost undisturbed in those years between the Mexican War and what was to come in 1861. While he was superintendent at West Point, his wife's mother, Mrs. Custis, died. Arlington became the Lees' residence, for the grieving Mr. Custis asked the family to make his home theirs. Colonel Lee didn't like the life of a school supervisor, even if that school was the Military Academy. He chafed for a more active army career, and so he was delighted when his old friend, now Secretary of War Jefferson Davis, appointed him colonel of a new cavalry regiment. Colonel Lee had remained only three years as the superintendent of West Point.

Lee's new regiment was assigned to Texas and to Texas went the new colonel, fruitlessly chasing raiding Indians and Mexican bandits along the wild Rio Grande. It was a lonely life and often a dull one, and his tour of duty in the far-away Western country was saddened by the death of his father-in-law.

Back to Virginia went Colonel Lee to his family and to the administration of the great but run-down Arlington holdings. The Army gave him leave and the leave lasted nearly two years. He was still at Arlington when he received the emergency order from the War Department to command the federal troops sent to quell John Brown's raid at Harpers Ferry.

And from that day on, the dark cloud of war, at first so small and then grown larger and larger, became a black shroud that hung over the United States. The reasonable men on both sides shook their heads. It is no use, they said, the hotheads are in command. Following Abraham Lincoln's election to the presidency of the United States, fiery South Carolina seceded from the Union in December, 1860. By that time most Americans feared that the Federal Union itself would be preserved or dissolved only after the shedding of American blood.

When South Carolina seceded, Lee again was in far-off Texas. He had been sent there to rejoin his Indian-chasing regiment and had been placed in command of the entire Southwest. Night after night he must have lain in his lonely tent wondering what was in store for his beloved state and for the country he served; and trying to make up his mind what he would do if the two should part. In the South, state after state began to follow South Carolina out of the Union. Robert E. Lee's anguish mounted. This is what he wrote to a cousin:

"God save us from our folly, selfishness and short-sightedness. What will be the result I cannot conjecture. I only see that a fearful calamity is upon us, and fear that the country will have to pass through for its sins a fiery ordeal. I am unable to realize that our people will destroy a government inaugurated by the blood and wisdom of our patriot fathers, that has given us peace and prosperity at home, power and security abroad.

"I wish to live under no other government, and there is no sacrifice I am not ready to make for the preservation of the Union save that of honor. If a disruption takes place, I shall go back to my native state and save in her defense there will be one soldier less in the world than now."

I will go back to my native state, Robert E. Lee had said, *and I will not fight unless she be invaded.*

He was not being a rebellious citizen when he wrote this. He had been taught all his life, even at West Point, that the United States was a voluntary gathering together of independent states. He did not believe that the Union should be dissolved, yet he thought that any state had the legal right to leave if it were foolish enough to want to do so. He did not wish Virginia or any other Southern state to quit the Union. But he would defend that right with his sword and his honor.

Lee expressed his thoughts in a letter to his son Custis

Only a few months before the outbreak of
the Civil War itself Lee wrote his thoughts to
his son Custis. In this letter he repeated his
fear of great calamity from the dissolving of
the Union and repeated that he would be willing to sacrifice everything but his honor to pre-
vent such disaster.

"Still," he said, "a Union that can be maintained only by swords and bayonets, if strife and civil war are to take the place of brotherly love and kindness, has no charm for me."

Matters went from bad to worse. Representatives of the seceding states of South Carolina, Georgia, Florida, Alabama, Mississippi, Louisiana and Texas met in Montgomery, Alabama, and set up a new nation on American soil, the Confederate States of America. Jefferson Davis, the former Secretary of War, was elected President.

"Good riddance," some people in the North said. Others only mourned the departure as an accomplished fact; but the rest demanded that the military might of the United States be used to force the seceding states back into the Federal union.

Few people talked of anything but war. Abraham Lincoln, the new President whose election had so enraged the Southern secessionists, first tried to bring about a peaceable settlement. Lincoln said that if he had to choose between a united nation with slavery or a disunited nation without it, he would choose the united nation.

But he did say also that no state had the right to secede from the Union. And President Lincoln backed up his words in April, 1861, by sending reinforcements to Fort Sumter in the harbor of Charleston, South Carolina. The South Carolina forces fired on Sumter and the war had begun. Lincoln called for 75,000 volunteers.

Early in 1861 before Fort Sumter was attacked, General Scott summoned his long-time favorite officer to Washington. It was no secret that he had a higher regard for Robert E. Lee than for any other officer in the United States Army. He considered him the nation's military genius.

Lee must have known what the aged hero had in mind. And he knew too what his answer would have to be. He had spent many a tortuous, soul-searching hour making his decision. They met in Washington on March 2, 1861—the Army's top-ranking general who had served his nation for more than fifty years and the younger man whom he considered his most likely successor.

"I want you to be second in command to me," General Scott said. That meant that Robert E. Lee would in fact lead the Union forces in war or peace, whichever lay ahead,

General Scott summoned his long-time favorite officer

for General Scott was far too old and over-
weight for active duty.

Gravely, the son of Virginia answered that
he was not prepared to accept.

But not yet was he forced to a final decision. Before the month was out his permanent commission as a colonel in the Army of the United States was delivered to him at Arlington. It bore the signature of the President whose election had led almost every Southern state to secede. Only Virginia still held back. That same day there arrived a letter from the new Confederate States of America asking Lee to accept a general's commission in its army. All that month he hesitated. He wanted to know what Virginia would do before he made up his mind. In April, the Virginia lawmakers met in their capitol in Richmond to reach the fateful decision. And once again Colonel Lee was summoned to the nation's capital to confer with Francis Blair, a close confidant of President Lincoln himself.

"Would you accept the field command of

the American armies with the rank of major general, sir?" Blair asked.

The historic moment of decision had come. In his mind's eye, Lee must have seen the fertile Valley of Virginia and the old sunlit homes of his ancestors; the shaded rivers and the shimmering blue mountains that he knew and loved. Northern forces, seeking to defeat the South, would have to strike at and through Virginia. Could he lead those armies through the ruins of his beloved state?

"I cannot, Mr. Blair," Lee said firmly. "If Virginia secedes, I will resign from the Army. I can take no part in an invasion of the Southern states. If Virginia is invaded, I will help defend her."

That very day Virginia seceded. Lee prayed and reflected for hours. Then he wrote a letter of resignation to General Scott. Soon afterward he accepted command of Virginia's troops.

In the same month Confederate artillery in Charleston opened fire on Fort Sumter after the commander of that island fortress in the harbor refused to surrender. The Southerners insisted that the North really started the war because President Lincoln had dispatched supplies to its garrison.

To the Lee family, the war meant immediate departure from Arlington, just across the river from Washington. General Lee wrote his wife that she must leave her ancestral home, and warned her to make plans for several years of war.

The daughter of George Washington Park Custis packed her most treasured personal belongings and the Washington family portraits, and superintended the burial of the family silver. She would come back to Arlington, she kept comforting herself. The war could not last forever, and surely the Union leaders would spare so famous an American shrine.

And spare it they did; but Mary Custis Lee never saw her father's home again. After the war, with senseless cruelty, the victorious Union government would forbid her ever to enter it. And throughout the war, worry would be her constant companion; anxiety not only for the safety of her husband but of the three sons who followed him—Custis, a first lieutenant in the regular army who resigned his commission to fight for the South; Rooney, Virginia planter, who led a troop of cavalry, and teen-age Robert, who joined up as an enlisted artilleryman.

And Robert E. Lee, who might have led the forces of the United States in that war, donned a uniform of gray in defense of his state.

He had searched his soul, he had sought the

answer to honor's way; and to his own satisfaction he had decided that his only course would be to fight in behalf of his state, the home of Washington and Jefferson and Madison and Monroe and his own father, Light-Horse Harry Lee, who had helped to win the nation's independence.

Now Robert E. Lee, Light-Horse Harry's son, was to lead the seceders from that nation in a long-lasting and devastating war. But it was not with the thought of personal gain that Lee made his decision. His sense of honor told him he had no other course.

7

The Hopeless Struggle

The road of honor becomes hidden now in
the smoke of battle and of burning homes. Beside it lie dead and wounded men, and the
soft Virginia air is bruised by their cries. Along
the road rides Major General Robert E. Lee,
of the Confederate States of America, grieving for the dead of Virginia and the South and

the warring brothers. But no man who saw him or who rode beside him or who trudged behind him has written or said that Robert E. Lee was ever anything but the kindly knight, the Christian soldier, and the gallant leader. Not once did men see him falter.

How was the South able to put up such a fight? Certainly not because the Southerners were as numerous as their foes. The population of the eleven seceding states numbered only five million whites and some four million Negro slaves. The twenty-one Union states had a population of twenty-three million and new immigrants constantly swelled it. The North had most of the industry, the shipping, the railroads and the money. The South, pinning its hopes on the world's need for cotton, had almost no industry, no great manufacturing centers. The South had almost no navy, and the Northern navy's success in blockading the Southern ports and preventing the shipment of cotton to Europe—and the return of needed war materials in exchange—played a large part in the South's defeat. Nor did the South have a monopoly on courage, for the bravery on both sides was epic. But the South did have three assets in a considerably greater degree than did the Union.

First of all, the average Southerner was more skilled in arms, more accustomed to the outdoors, and more at home in the saddle and in the forest and field than were his Northern kinsmen. It was a difference between countryman and city dweller, and between frontiersman and settled farmer. Then, too, it was the Southerners' sad lot to do almost all their fighting in their homeland; and brave men always fight harder when their own firesides and families are threatened.

But the South won battle after battle, and held out for four years chiefly because of the men who led her armies. The profession of arms had long been admired and followed in the South where a military tradition existed especially among the planter families. Among the South's professional soldiers who followed their states in secession, an unusual number were highly gifted in the grim art of war. Wherever students of warfare gather even now, the careers and battle plans of the rampaging cavalrymen Jeb Stuart and Nathan Bedford Forest, of Stonewall Jackson, of Albert Sidney Johnston and Joe Johnston and Pierre Beauregard and many another Southern general are studied and admired. And above them all, the generalship of Robert E. Lee, whose military genius has been reckoned the nation's finest, is most looked up to by military men the world over.

But General Lee, Confederate States of America, did not win either public fame or honors in front line combat during his first year as a soldier of the South. Mississippi's Jefferson Davis, the newly elected President of the Confederate States of America, knew Lee's ability as well as had the North's General Scott who offered him the command of the Union forces. So President Davis summoned Lee to Richmond, Virginia, where the new nation's capital had been established and made him a ranking member of his own staff. Robert E. Lee, the staff strategist, planned where the Confederates should make their first determined stand against the invading North, a little place in his beloved Virginia only a few miles from Washington, named Manassas Junction.

But he was not at Manassas on July 21, 1861, when the first great battle of the war ended in a tremendous Confederate victory. To his disappointment, President Davis kept him in Richmond, doing vital staff work. So it was Jackson—who got his nickname "Stonewall" here for holding his forces immovable against enemy assault—and Beauregard and Joe Johnston who won deserved honors for driving the Federal forces off the field and all the way back to Washington in a rout. A few fresh troops and sufficient cavalry and the Confederates might have captured Washington itself that day. Perhaps they might have ended the war almost as soon as it began.

"I wished to participate in the battle and am

mortified at my absence," General Lee wrote Mrs. Lee. "But the President thought it more important that I should be here. I could not have done as well as has been done but I could have helped and taken part in a struggle for our homes and neighbors."

But while victory was the South's at Manassas, the Union forces were making headway in the mountains of western Virginia, and it was there that Lee was soon sent. His army was plagued with measles, and Lee was plagued with slow-acting and quarreling subordinate officers. Partly because he was unwilling to act harshly enough toward these quarreling generals, the Confederate campaign in western Virginia ended in failure.

Lee himself was strongly criticized in the Southern press. Some even called him "Evacuating Lee." Years later the general recalled with quiet indignation, "We appointed all our worst generals to command the army and all our best generals to edit the newspapers."

A real personal loss in the campaign was the death of Colonel John Augustine Washington, great-nephew of the first President, who rode with Lee as a volunteer aide. He was ambushed and killed while scouting the enemy.

"The righteous perish," wrote the saddened General Lee. "May God have mercy on us all."

It was a discouraged commander who rode back to Richmond on what was to become perhaps the most famous of war horses, his loved Traveller, the staunch, gray thoroughbred he had acquired in the mountains and who would be his favorite mount throughout the war. "Marse" Robert and Traveller together brought tears and cheers and renewed determination to many a ragged Confederate throughout the war and afterward.

Lee was not long in Richmond. The defenses of Charleston and Savannah needed strengthening so to these cities he went. Long ago his first assignment as an officer in the United States Army had been to the defenses of Savannah. Now he was to strengthen its fortifications against the forces he had once helped lead.

The North's superior resources began to tell as soon as it recovered from the defeat at Manassas. Within the year the Union began to win victories. President Davis, whose conduct of the war was being increasingly criticized, placed General Lee in charge of military operations of the Armies of the Confederacy in June, 1862.

If Lee actually had been given complete authority, the war might have had a different ending. In reality President Davis continued overall direction of the Confederate forces. Lee's real task, and one he performed with amazing ability, was to protect Richmond, the capital, as commander of the Army of Northern Virginia. This he did for three years, winning victory after victory, until the superior strength and equal courage of the North resulted in the crushing of the South.

The Confederates won battles elsewhere than in Virginia and fought the Yankee foemen to a standstill in many another engagement during those three years. But a draw was as good as a victory for the Union which could afford to lose man for man and gun for gun against the outnumbered Rebels and still come out on top. And the South's defeats were especially costly for they came on Southern soil, where its own small resources could be destroyed.

When General Lee returned to Richmond, his first thought was to reunite his family. He had not seen his wife and daughters for a year. His three sons were in the Confederate Army. Mrs. Lee and the girls were staying at a kinsman's plantation home, the White House, on the Pamunkey River. As soon as General Lee found a house, he wrote her to come to Richmond.

Mrs. Lee was a resourceful woman. When she left the White House ahead of the Union Army's advance, she tacked a note to the door. It read "Northern soldiers who profess to rev-

He rode back to Richmond on his loved horse Traveller

erence Washington, forbear to desecrate the home of his first married life, the property of his wife, now owned by her descendants."

General McClellan, the Union commander, honored her plea, but not long afterward Federal soldiers burned the historic mansion. Before that wrongful deed, Mrs. Lee was herself taken prisoner. But war followed certain rules of decent conduct in those days. General McClellan sent the wife of his opponent to the Confederate lines, so Mary Lee was soon reunited in Richmond with her soldier husband and her three fighting sons.

General Lee did not have much time for family reunions. His face was beginning to betray his anxiety. A sorrowing look could be detected in his eyes; and the beard that he had newly grown was becoming thickly flecked with white.

He had reason to be anxious. Almost everywhere the Union was forging ahead. By the end of April, 1862, New Orleans, far to the South, had fallen to Farragut's gunboats, plowing up the Mississippi from the Gulf. Ulysses S. Grant, a new and almost unknown Northern general about whom the nation and the world were later to hear much, struck through Tennessee capturing Forts Henry and Donelson. In a bloody battle on April 6 and 7, 1862, at Shiloh Landing on the Tennessee River he had dealt such losses to the Southern forces that although the battle was at the least a draw for the Confederates, the outnumbered Southerners had retreated. And in Virginia, General George B. McClellan, whom Lee had known in the Mexican War, was leading 115,000 men. They had been brought down by ship to march on Richmond, the Confederate capital, by way

On her way to Richmond, Mrs. Lee was taken prisoner

of the Virginia peninsula between the York and James rivers. Confederate supplies were low. The blue-clad Union troops were threatening the Confederate capital itself.

And now Robert E. Lee showed what he could do for his state and the new Southern nation whose cause he had espoused. President Davis had already put him in charge of all military operations under Davis' own direction; and when at the Battle of Seven Pines Lee's dear friend General Joe Johnston was wounded, President Davis rode through the night with Lee and told him it was now his primary assignment to protect Richmond.

The Union armies were moving in on Richmond from three sides. Against them Lee had only 80,000 men, and at the closest point the enemy was only seven miles from Richmond. If the Confederacy was to last, the three Union armies, vastly superior in numbers, must be turned back.

With the utmost daring, Lee decided to strike instead of to wait on the defensive. He would first march quickly northward through the Valley of Virginia, and try to destroy the Union forces there. If that plan succeeded, he was sure that President Lincoln would withdraw the second Union army, which was at

Fredericksburg, fifty miles from Richmond, in the belief that Washington itself would be threatened. That would leave only the Third Army, commanded by his old comrade, General McClellan.

To thrust northward through the valley, Lee called upon another military genius, Thomas J. Jackson, a one-time professor at Virginia Military Institute. Stonewall Jackson's "Foot Cavalry" sped up and down the valley, defeating three Federal forces. Lincoln's Secret Service overestimated the size of the Rebel Army, and the North reacted as Lee thought it would. Lincoln ordered the withdrawal of the forces at Fredericksburg, and Lee turned on McClellan—"Little Mac"—with Jackson rushing back down the valley to help.

Now Lee summoned a soldier who was the young lieutenant accompanying Lee at Harpers Ferry. He was General Jeb Stuart now, one of the most intrepid cavalrymen of all times. Stuart rode completely around McClellan's army, captured and burned millions of dollars' worth of Yankee supplies, and returned with the report for which Lee was waiting. He knew where the Union forces were and what they had, and he was ready to hit them.

McClellan had not dreamed that the Confederates would attack his superior force, and he had divided his army. Part of it was on one side of the Chickahominy River, which flows into the James, and part on the other. For seven days Lee ripped the separated Federal forces, first on one side of the Chickahominy and again on the other. McClellan's men, badly defeated, retreated and dug in to wait another chance. Lee and Jackson in one month had saved Richmond when it had been given up

Gen. J.E.B. Stuart

by almost everyone. They had done it with a greatly outnumbered army. And Lee had revealed for the first time the quality of daring that would mark him throughout the war. To his men and to the South he was an idol.

President Lincoln called on another Union general, a braggart named John Pope, who was confident he could defeat Lee. But Lee and Jackson boldly attacked and, in the Second Battle of Manassas, inflicted one of the worst defeats of the war on the Union forces. Again the Yankees ran back to Washington, leaving undreamed-of riches in food, arms and supplies for the hungry Confederates.

Here was the high-water mark of the Confederacy. The victorious, ragged Rebels quickly invaded Maryland on Pope's heels. This invasion, Lee knew, would take pressure off of Virginia, and a victory or two might bring peace.

For the first time, a Southern army was in Northern territory. But what an army! Half of its foot soldiers were barefooted, and scarcely a man was fully uniformed. They were fighting and marching on empty stomachs, on stomachs aching from eating green fruit and parched corn. Men without shoes, Lee decided, could not take part in the invasion; and this meant that his Army would be reduced by thousands. But if the Rebels were low on clothes and food, they were high in spirits. They were carrying the fight to the enemy! The Confederate bands blared "Maryland, My Maryland," "Dixie" and "The Bonny Blue Flag" as Stonewall Jackson's men led the fording of the Potomac.

And what did they look like to the foe? To one Northern observer, they were "dirty, lank, ugly specimens of humanity, with shocks of hair sticking through the holes in their hats, and the dust thick on their dirty faces, these men who had driven back again and again our splendid legions. . . . I must confess that I felt humiliated at the thought that this horde of ragamuffins could set our grand army of the

Union at defiance. It seems as if a single regiment of our gallant boys in blue could drive this dirty crew in the river without any trouble. But I wish you could see how they behaved—a crowd of boys on a holiday don't seem happier. They are on the broad grin all the time."

The high spirits of these grinning ragamuffins had been dampened at the beginning of the pursuit of Pope when General Lee, sitting on a log with Traveller's reins twisted about his arm, was thrown heavily to the ground when his steed reared. Both of Lee's wrists were badly sprained. He led his army in an ambulance for a few days.

The army raced ahead. They camped at Frederick, Maryland, for a day, and then on September 9, 1862, the Confederates prepared to advance into Pennsylvania.

The Rebels were low on clothes and

Four days later General McClellan, unaware of what Lee was up to or how many men he had, entered the town of Frederick. And then occurred one of those unbelievable events that change the course of history.

In packing up, one of Lee's staff officers dropped a packet of cigars, wrapped in a copy of the orders telling Lee's whole plan of the

hey were certainly high in spirits

campaign. They were found and taken to General McClellan.

With this information, particularly the disclosure that Lee had divided his army, McClellan struck at Antietam. He had 87,000 men; Lee and Jackson together had only 35,000. For two days the men of the Union and the Confederacy fought and died in one of the costliest battles in all history. The Confederates, strung out between the Potomac River and Antietam Creek, repulsed attack after attack; Stonewall Jackson held one flank, General D. H. Hill the center and General James Longstreet the other flank. At one point the Federal forces almost overran Lee's men, but just at this juncture, a division which had been left at Harpers Ferry by Jackson after its capture on September 15th, arrived and saved the day. They drove the Federal forces down the little hill where the heart of the attack was being made. The next day neither army was in shape to fight, and that night Lee retreated to Virginia.

Had it not been for the lost orders, it is more than possible that the Confederate invasion might have forced the Union to sue for peace.

Those bloody days of September 16 and 17,

1862, were perhaps the most fateful in all of the history of the United States. From then on the Confederates never had a real chance for a draw. General McClellan himself wrote that if he had been defeated at Antietam, Lee could have marched to Washington, Baltimore, Philadelphia and New York. "The Confederates," said McClellan, "could have levied supplies from a fertile and undevastated country, extorted a tribute from wealthy and populous cities, and nowhere east of the Alleghenies was there another organized force able to arrest its march."

But it didn't happen that way. And it is best for all Americans that it did not.

8

To Gettysburg and Appomattox

If 1862 had been a bad year for the Confederacy, 1863 was to be worse. It wasn't that the South didn't win its share of the battles, but these victories brought her no closer to winning a war.

Southern fighting spirit was no match for the resources, the superior numbers and the powerful blockading navy of the North. By the spring of 1863 the Union Armies were over-running almost every region of the South.

Only Lee remained unbeatable. He had defeated a tremendous Union Army again in the winter of 1862 at Fredericksburg when General Burnside led 120,000 men toward Richmond. Lee's men entrenched themselves on the slopes behind the town of Fredericksburg. Four times the courageous Union troops sought to storm the gray lines on Marye's Hill and Stafford Heights. Four times they were thrown back with slaughter so great that the Confederates themselves cheered the bravery of the men in blue. Lee's pride in his men in this victory led him to say that day, "It is well that war is so terrible or we should grow too fond of it."

Again in the spring of 1863 Lee turned back the Union Army, trying for a third time to capture Richmond. In a tangled land of swamps and forests and swift flowing streams which well merited the name it had—the Wilderness —Lee and Jackson and the Virginia mud combined to administer to General Hooker and his men the worst defeat the Federal forces were to suffer in the whole war. But for Lee it was a defeat in victory. On the night of May 2nd gallant Stonewall Jackson was mistakenly shot by his own men. His wounded left arm was amputated in an effort to save his life. "Jackson has lost only his left arm," Lee wrote when he heard the surgeon had removed it. "But I have lost my right." A few days later Jackson died. It was the worst loss of leadership that the South was to suffer.

Soon thereafter Lee's son Rooney was severely wounded in a major cavalry battle; and while recovering in a friend's home he was captured. In the winter of 1863-64, he was sent home as an exchange prisoner and fought in the closing campaigns of the war.

After the Wilderness victory General Lee determined to carry the attack once more to the enemy. Amassing 75,000 men, the largest force the Confederacy had yet brought together, he struck out again across the Potomac for Pennsylvania, the heartland of the North. What was he planning to do? Not to conquer but to ease enemy pressure on Virginia, and secure provisions for his men. Explained an aide later, "He expected to move about, maneuver and alarm the enemy, threaten their cities, hit any blows he might be able to deliver without risking a general battle and then, toward fall, return and recover his base."

Perhaps the Federal armies would not only cease their pressure on Richmond and rush those forces back to protect Washington, but the Union might even withdraw the troops that were besieging Vicksburg on the Mississippi. And that would be a Southern victory too, for unless Vicksburg fell, the North could

Gen. Thomas J. Jackson

not succeed in Grant's primary objective of splitting the Confederacy by securing control of the whole lower Mississippi River.

Lee was conscious by now that the South

had almost no hope of winning the war. He urged President Davis to encourage the peace party that was growing up in the North; and he hoped by the Pennsylvania invasion to influence those Northerners who were weary of fighting and desired peace. He advised President Davis just before marching into Pennsylvania that "the North's numbers, resources and all the means and appliances for carrying on the war made the South reliant only on heaven's mercy." Then he set out to try to perform miracles in Pennsylvania.

There, deep in enemy country, Lee made a fateful mistake. In those days before aerial observation and our present swift means of communication, a general relied on his cavalry to discover the whereabouts of the enemy. Lee gave unclear instructions to his famous cavalry leader, Jeb Stuart, who twice before had circled entire armies of the enemy and returned with much information and booty. So Stuart, who loved daring deeds, went galloping off at the head of his men, intent on turning the trick again.

From then on Lee did not know where the enemy was. He didn't see Stuart again until July 2nd when the battle of Gettysburg was half over and all but lost. To make things worse, the Union forces captured a messenger from President Davis, bearing Davis' refusal to approve a plan of Lee's for a small reserve Confederate force to make a threat against Washington and cause Federal troops to return to protect the capital. The Union leader, General Hooker, knew then that he had nothing to fear in his own rear. The third blow to the Confederates came with the appointment of General George Meade to replace Hooker.

And this brings us to Gettysburg where the most momentous battle on American soil was fought.

The strangest thing about this most famous of American battles is that no one on either side planned to fight at Gettysburg at all. The opposing armies practically stumbled upon each other on the edge of the little Pennsylvania town, whose name was to become symbolic of human endurance and gallantry and of the floodtide of the Confederacy. A handful of famished Confederates wandered toward the pretty little town, looking for food and shoes and whatever they could find. This advance force ran into a band of Union cavalrymen and the shooting started. Alarmed by the gunfire, reinforcements on each side rushed into combat and before long sizeable numbers of men were engaged.

General Meade drew up his forces in a long fishhook curve on the crests of rolling slopes south of Gettysburg, elevations whose names will live forever in American history—Big Round Top and Little Round Top, Devil's Den, Cemetery Ridge and many another— places where the children of Gettysburg had played and explored. Along Seminary Ridge the Confederates prepared for the attack.

On Cemetery Ridge—and it was well named —the soldiers of the North waited. Fortunately for them, Union troops had been able the first day of battle to seize Little Round Top and Big Round Top, two small hills which dominated the region.

The Confederate assault to drive them off these strategic hills on the second day was late in getting started. Longstreet, who led the attack, was unable to dislodge the Federals.

138

On and on they charged, with General Armistead in
the vanguard waving his cap upon his sword

On the third day Lee prepared to risk all in a massed attack against the Union lines on Cemetery Ridge, and it was then that the most heartbreaking charge in all American history took place. Lee ordered General George Pickett to lead his Virginians across the open fields against the foe.

Fifteen thousand men advanced against hopeless odds, toward massed artillery and waiting infantry, across fields reddened with their blood. But they would not halt or retreat. On and on they charged, their leader, General Armistead, in the vanguard waving his cap upon his sword. For a few fleeting moments the battle flag of the Confederacy waved on Cemetery Ridge. Beneath the waving banners a handful of surviving Confederates battled with steel and fists and rocks against the thousands of waiting Union soldiers. Then it was over. And with the failure of Pickett's charge, the Confederacy had lost its last chance to gain an honorable peace.

And what did General Robert E. Lee say, although he might have blamed his subordinate Longstreet, among others?

"All this has been my fault. It is I who have lost this fight, and you must help me out of it the best way you can."

To President Davis, who knew better, Lee wrote that he alone was to blame. The Army of Northern Virginia retreated across the Potomac. No man followed it. The victorious Union had had enough of fighting for a while too.

And this was the beginning of the end. The morale of the people at home was shattered. Lincoln had proclaimed that the slaves were free on January 1, 1863, and the Union Armies were being strengthened by tens of thousands of Negro recruits. Near the war's end the South tried with little success to persuade its former slaves to enlist under the Confederate banner. The South's politicians were falling out among themselves. It was almost impossible for Lee to get further recruits. His soldiers were starving, in rags, sick and almost shelterless, but so great was their reputation and so hard the blows they had struck that not throughout 1863 did the Yankees try to attack the Army of Northern Virginia.

Elsewhere the North pushed the fight. Vicksburg had fallen on July 4, 1863, the day that Lee began his retreat from Gettysburg, and the Northern soldiers swarmed throughout the mid-South. Then in the early spring of 1864 a notable general named William Tecumseh Sherman, who loved the South but loved the Union

more, thrust toward Atlanta, destroying everything in his path.

Once again the North thrust toward Richmond, the heart of the Confederacy. This time
it was Ulysses S. Grant who led where Mc-
Clellan and Polk and Burnside and Hooker
had failed. No longer able to mount an attack,
Robert E. Lee stood on the defensive. He was
pinning his hopes on the peace party in the
North. If he could just keep fighting, maybe
the North would be willing to call it a draw.

But U. S. Grant, whom some called the
Butcher and who later was to be President of
the United States, was no man to want the
contest to end without victory for the Union.
Grant wouldn't quit pushing. He didn't have
to. He had so many men that in 1864 he could
have lost three soldiers for every one Confederate and still have won the contest. Wear them

out, he seemed to say, wear them out. And the South was so badly worn that it could not withstand another sledge-hammer assault. Or so it seemed to many Southerners in that despairing spring of 1864.

Once again General Lee decided to meet the enemy in the dense Wilderness country where he had sent General Hooker reeling back in defeat. He placed his men in a sixty-mile line that reached from the Rapidan River on the north to just a few miles above Richmond, mostly in the same tangled growth which had bewildered and helped defeat the Union forces before.

For a month, the bloodiest month of the entire war, Grant tried to break through the line that alone stood between him and Richmond. Each time Lee's smaller forces drove back the Federal troops. He had only 60,000 men to Grant's more than 120,000. But he turned them back time and again—at Spotsylvania, at Hanover Court House, at Cold Harbor and many another site.

At Spotsylvania Court House the Federal troops briefly tore through a thinly manned section of the Confederate line. General Lee galloped up on Traveller and made ready to lead a counterattack himself. One of his generals, John Gordon, urged him to go back. The Virginians and Georgians surrounding their commander cried to him, "General Lee to the rear, Lee to the rear," and shouted that they would not charge until he sought the comparative safety behind them.

General Gordon turned Traveller aside and led his men to the attack. Lee galloped off for reinforcements and returned them to the scene of the fighting. Once more he faced toward the

"General Lee to the rear, Lee to the rear!"

enemy, and again the cry of the Confederates
went up: "Go back, General, go back."

"Drive them away and I will go back," said
Lee. Shouting the Rebel yell, the men in

ragged butternut and gray drove the Federals off the field.

In the one month of May, Grant lost 50,000 troops. He made one more attempt, at Cold Harbor, to break the lower end of the Confederate line. Almost every available Union soldier charged the Confederate trenches, only to be driven back again and again until 10,-000 of them lay dead and wounded.

That was the end of the Wilderness campaign. The Union Army had lost 60,000 men, as many as the total number of Confederates under Lee.

But this tremendous victory could not stop Grant. He had many more men and he had the determination to win. Once more he moved on Richmond, this time coming up from the south, centering his forces on Petersburg.

And now Lee could not look for help from

elsewhere. General Sherman was rampaging through Georgia, leaving desolation in his wake. All of Tennessee had fallen. The Army of Northern Virginia was shrinking, as the sick and faint-hearted deserted in increasing numbers, while their stronger or more gallant comrades fell to Northern bullets and disease which ravaged their underfed, underclothed ranks.

By the spring of 1865 it was all but over. Only 40,000 hungry men made up the Army of Northern Virginia. From the South, Sherman was raging out of Georgia to join forces with Grant. Together they would have at least five times as many men as did Lee.

Robert E. Lee made one last attack in an attempt to break through Grant's lines. When his men were unable to carry out his plan, through sheer exhaustion and lack of numbers,

Lee reported the worst to President Davis.

"We must retreat," he said. "Richmond must fall to the enemy." It was for him a tragic climax to the three years during which he had magnificently repulsed the enemy armies every time they sought to capture the Confederate capital.

Lee led his little force west, seeking refuge in the mountains in the hope that he could join later with whatever was left of the Confederate armies which had been defeated in the lower South. As he retreated, somehow somebody in his command failed to have even the most meager supplies waiting at Amelia Court House, as ordered for his men, at the end of the arduous two-day march. During the retreat Lee's son Custis was captured, the second of the boys to be taken. When the Confederates halted to look around for food, their retreat was cut off by overwhelming forces of Northern cavalry.

In the midst of these difficulties, a letter arrived from Grant asking Lee to surrender. Sadly Lee conferred with his generals, then wrote to General Grant to learn his terms. The tiny village of Appomattox Court House was designated as the place for the meeting on April 9th of the two commanders; and toward a red brick house in the village Lee rode on Traveller, resplendent in the only full-dress uniform which remained to him. If he were to be made a prisoner of General Grant, he told his officers, he wanted to look his best. And look his best the grim-faced, haggard warrior did, his cavalry boots shining, his sword magnificently housed in a gleaming scabbard, and a colorful sash around his waist. Ulysses Grant wore only a private's uniform, his trousers muddy, and he bore no designation of rank except the general's stars on his shoulder straps.

General Grant was generous in victory. He did not ask for the sword of his defeated opponent. He permitted the Confederate officers to retain their side arms, and told Lee his men could take their thin horses home for the spring planting. He sent food from his own stores to the hungry Confederates and refused to let his own troops cheer or shoot in celebration of the triumph. You can read the full heart-warming story of the surrender at Appomattox in another Landmark Book, *Lee and Grant at Appomattox.*

Three days after the meeting in the little house at Appomattox Court House, the Army of Northern Virginia surrendered.

History has recorded no greater loyalty and

love than the defeated men of the South showed their fallen commander. As he rode back among them, his eyes blinded with tears, these scarecrow soldiers shouted themselves hoarse, telling their general that they would keep on fighting for him, touching his horse, his boots, halting Traveller so that they could speak to him, and sobbing without control.

On April 10th, General Robert E. Lee issued his last official statement to his men, an address of farewell:

"After four years of arduous service, marked by unsurpassed courage and fortitude, the Army of Northern Virginia has been compelled to yield to overwhelming numbers and resources.

"I need not tell the survivors of so many hard-fought battles, who have remained steadfast to the last, that I have consented to this result through no distrust of them; but, feeling that valour and devotion could accomplish nothing that could compensate for the loss that would have attended the continuation of the contest, I have determined to avoid the useless sacrifice of those whose past services have endeared them to their countrymen.

"By the terms of agreement, officers and men can return to their homes and remain there until exchanged.

"You will take with you the satisfaction that proceeds from the consciousness of duty faithfully performed; and I earnestly pray that a merciful God will extend to you His blessing and protection.

They would keep fighting for him, Lee's men shouted

"With an unceasing admiration of
your constancy and devotion to your
country, and a grateful remembrance
of your kind and generous considera-

tion of myself, I bid you all an affec-
tionate farewell."

The Army of Northern Virginia was dead.
So was the Confederacy.

9

The Young Men Must Build

What do defeated men turn to after four years of bloodshed?

For the enlisted men and junior officers there was only one answer. They simply turned homeward, too often only to fallen bricks and ashes, and set about the task of keeping body and soul together. But the ranking officers debated among themselves, and their decisions were not the same nor were they easy.

They could not be sure for a considerable time after Appomattox whether or not they would be tried as traitors. Some, in despair, took ships to foreign lands and offered their military services to strange governments. A few never returned to the United States. Others withdrew in bitterness to make a living as best they could and to write their memories of the great battles. Some could be seen plowing fields that spring with the war horses that had borne them in battle.

The big question to the worn people of the South was "What will General Lee do?" President Jefferson Davis lay in a Federal prison; Lee was the leader in defeat to whom the thousands looked for guidance.

And so it was that General Lee's first decision after Appomattox went a long way toward beginning the healing of the old, deep wounds. He took an oath of allegiance to the United States government which he fought so long. And, turning down foreign military offers that must have been tempting, General Lee decided to stay with his state. In those first few days after the stunning reality of surrender he planned only on retiring to some distant farm to forget the past.

"I am looking for some little quiet house in the woods," he said to a friend, "where I can procure shelter and my daily bread if permitted by the victor. I wish to get Mrs. Lee out of Richmond as soon as practicable."

He was right in wanting to get both Mrs. Lee and himself out of the city. They were constantly sought out by people who loved them, people wanting favors, people wishing only to shake the hand of their old leader and to offer their services. Lee was besieged night and day in Richmond, not as a defeated general but as the hero of his people. But he had to make a living.

Soon he had a visitor from tiny Washington College, which was situated in Lexington, Virginia. To Robert E. Lee's surprise this spokesman offered him the presidency of the college. It wasn't much of a school, to be sure, and the salary of $1500 a year wasn't much salary. Washington College had almost no students because of the war, and its buildings had been gutted by Northern raiders.

But the general who had led Southern youth into battle didn't hesitate. This was his duty; the road of honor would lead now from Appomattox to a college campus where the young men of the South could be trained for leadership in time of peace.

Lee worried only that his wartime command of the Southern forces would bring down on the little school the wrath of the Northerners who could not yet find it in their hearts to forgive or forget. But he set that fear aside; and soon he wrote a letter of acceptance to Washington College.

Never did so notable a man take over the administration of so poverty-stricken and nearly hopeless a little institution. In 1864 Federal soldiers had destroyed the Washington College library, broken up its laboratory equipment, looted each of the beautiful red brick buildings, and burned the nearby Virginia Military Institute. The buildings were in bad disrepair. In the last year of the war only forty-five very young students and two professors were present. But that meant a greater challenge to Lee.

The happy trustees of Washington College drew up an announcement: "In dedicating his future life to the holy work of educating the youth of his country, General Lee presents a new and interesting phase of his grand and heroic character, a character than which no more perfect model exists among living men. . . . Let the young men of the country, North as well as South, be wise and profit not less by his precepts than by his great example."

In September of 1865, just five months after his surrender, General Lee mounted Traveller and rode alone from Richmond to Lexington, 108 miles away. He was dressed in a gray Confederate uniform, from which Confederate buttons and insignia had been removed, as ordered by the Federal government. As he rode he was

His 180-mile journey was like a triumphal procession

recognized everywhere, and his journey was almost a triumphal procession.

On October 2nd he was inaugurated as president of Washington College, which after his death was to be renamed Washington and Lee in his memory. From that day until his death, five years later, Robert E. Lee devoted all his energies to making the small university a place where Southern men could learn more than could be found in books alone. He taught them what was closest to his heart also, the meaning of honor in their dealings with one another and with the faculty and with their fellow citizens.

Never has any college president worked harder and at more varied tasks than did General Lee. He was his own clerk and secretary. He supervised the remodeling and improvements of the grounds. He visited every class in the growing student body each day. Although he hated to ask for money from anyone, he took part in the successful efforts to raise funds for the college. It is good to know that even so soon after the bitterness of war many thousands of dollars came in from Northern friends of Lee and of Virginia.

Most important in the education of the students, he added a number of practical subjects to the six courses—Latin, Greek, mathematics, philosophy, political economy, and natural philosophy (chemistry and physics)—that were already being taught. The new courses were practical chemistry, agricultural chemistry, practical mechanics, mechanical drawing and architecture, applied mathematics, and French, German, Spanish, Italian, modern history and English literature.

The student body of fifty who registered on the first day of the session in 1865 grew to more than one hundred by 1866 and over 400 in 1867. The faculty expanded, too. And though there was always need for more money than the little college could find, the endowment funds and

the gifts multiplied so that at least it could oper-
ate on more than a month-to-month basis.

Always Lee counseled the students and his
fellow citizens of Virginia to work for peace, and
to try to forget their old hatreds of the foe. Once

"You cannot be a true man until you learn to obey"

in 1866 he halted a mob of angry Virginia farmers from lynching a horse thief. Time and again he averted clashes between his hot-headed young students and members of the Federal forces that were still stationed in Lexington. Sorely troubled by the vengeful attitude which politicians in the North were beginning to take toward the defeated South, he counseled his friends to support the government that, two years after the war, seemed unwilling to let them return as equal citizens. He carried on, without a secretary, a widespread correspondence with old veterans, with friends in the service, with widows of dead Confederates, with all who came to him for help or advice. Once he was asked whether he thought he had to answer all such letters.

"I certainly do," he said. "Think of these poor people. It is a great deal of trouble for them to write. Why should I not be willing to take the trouble to answer them? And as that is all I can give most of them, I give it ungrudgingly."

He was proud of the way the great majority of "his boys" lived up to his standards. "Study hard," he told them, "be always a gentleman, live cleanly and remember God, and be peaceable." Those rules would serve well in any time.

"You cannot be a true man," he told rebellious students, "until you learn to obey."

Never in those years as a teacher did he lose pride in the army he had led. Once he cautioned a brilliant student, a veteran of the Army of Northern Virginia, that he was working too hard.

"I am impatient, sir," the student answered. "I want to make up for the time I lost in the war."

"Never say that again," General Lee said, almost angrily. "However long you live and what-

ever you accomplish, you will find that the time
you spent in the Confederate army was the most
profitably spent portion of your life."

10

Soldier's End

During the autumn and winter of 1869, General Lee must have known that death, the conqueror whom he had met unafraid a thousand times, was beckoning to him.

That year the health of the tired warrior began to fail. Constantly he was in pain from rheumatism and a heart ailment, and the straight body of the soldier had begun to stoop badly.

He was only sixty-two years old but the hard four years in the saddle, the strain of war and its deep sorrows, and the pace at which he drove himself at Washington College had made him old before his time.

In the spring of 1870 he was so ill and tired that he decided to retire for a while from his college duties. With his daughter Agnes he visited his sons and the grave of Annie, the daughter who had died, and took a tour through the South for his health. But the tour turned out to be at least as wearing as his work, for everywhere the worshiping Southerners gathered to greet him; and his sense of duty and loyalty to these followers would not permit him to disappoint them.

After the tour was over that spring, he was unable to continue actively as college president.

The devoted trustees of Washington College urged him to take a long rest. He did so, throughout the summer, and in September he was able to greet the students and faculty in the chapel at the formal opening of the college session. Three days later he rounded out his fifth year as president of the little school to which he had come when it had all but closed down, and which he had molded into one of the finest institutions in the South.

Near the end of September he attended a faculty meeting. The next day he again went to his office on a cold wet day; and that afternoon, September 28th, he attended a meeting of the vestrymen of Grace Church. His last act as a churchman was a generous one. The vestry wanted to raise the rector's salary and each contributed to the amount needed; but when they

Cold and tired, he walked through the rain to his home

counted the money it was fifty-five dollars short of their goal. "I will give that sum," General Lee said.

It was night when the vestry meeting was

over, and, cold and worn out he walked through the rainy darkness to his home. There he collapsed. He was so sick that his family and physicians decided he could not be moved from the dining room, where he had been smitten.

For two weeks the brave old soldier fought death. Devotedly Mary Custis Lee, herself never well since the birth of their youngest child, nursed him. Sometimes he was delirious, sometimes he seemed to be mending. Then on the morning of October 11th he began to dream of battle. He gave orders to his old generals. "Tell Hill he must come up!" he said as strongly as if he were giving an order in the field. And then on the morning of October 12th, Robert E. Lee spoke his last words. "Strike the tent," he said. His life story was over.

But the story of Lee of Virginia does not have

an end, not so long as men respect and remember courage and high purpose and a sense of duty and honor. These qualities the leader of the rebellious Confederacy, a great American, had in as boundless a measure as any man. These traits are what he is remembered by, and should be. Today there is no North or South as far as dangerously violent divisions are concerned. There is no slavery in America to taunt the consciences of men. There is no longer any question that the United States is and will remain one indivisible nation. And one noble proof of our nation's unity is that all Americans, North and South, revere the memory of the Virginia cavalier whose military genius might have made the United States two countries. His failure saved us. His greatness remains.

Had Lee's sense of duty and honor not persuaded him that his first loyalty was to his state, and had he taken command of the Union armies, as offered, he might have been the nation's President in the peace that followed. His adversary, the indomitable Ulysses S. Grant, went on to become President; and there is no reason to disbelieve that Robert E. Lee might have been so honored had he taken the command that eventually was Grant's. But he chose the way his conscience told him to go, the way of Virginia, the state that the Lees and the Carters had served so long and well. And to Virginia's rebuilding he turned when the war ended, dedicating the rest of his life to training the sons of Virginia and the South for peacetime service to their states and the reunited nation.

Today the lovely town of Lexington, Virginia, is a mecca for Americans and the chapel at Washington and Lee University, where Lee lies buried, is a shrine. The cadets of nearby Virginia Military Institute, where the great Stonewall Jackson once taught, salute as they pass the chapel, and men enter his burial crypt as if it were a hallowed place.

That is as it should be. We remember Robert E. Lee, and Abraham Lincoln whom he defied, and Jefferson Davis under whom he served, and Ulysses S. Grant, the generous victor whom he fought so stubbornly and long, and Stonewall Jackson who was his right arm, and the gallant rest, the men in blue and in gray who followed these. We must never forget them, neither the men of the victorious North nor of the defeated South. Together, they made us what we are. Their sorrowful division led in time to our inseparable union. Their gallantry is our common inheritance, whether our ancestors lost with Lee or won with Grant.

And most of all Robert E. Lee represents

for all Americans the virtues we so greatly cherish and so greatly need. They are old ones but in our times they seem new.

A sense of honor and duty . . .

Love of family . . .

Pride in homeland. . . .

Devotion to God.

Index

179

John Askling, Indexer